# The Language of Flowers

### Penhaligon's
### Scented Treasury
### of Verse and
### Prose

Ex Libris

........................................................

# THE LANGUAGE OF FLOWERS

SHEILA PICKLES

HARMONY BOOKS
NEW YORK

For my Mother and Sister
In loving memory of my Father

# INTRODUCTION

Love's language may be talked with these;
To work out choicest sentences
No blossoms can be meeter;
And, such being used in Eastern bowers,
Young maids may wonder if the flowers
Or meanings be the sweeter.

ELIZABETH BARRETT BROWNING, 1806–1861

Dear Reader,

What could be more pleasurable than receiving an
unexpected bunch of flowers? A bunch of bluebells to
brighten a breakfast tray, Lily of the Valley to celebrate
May Day or a simple posy of wild honeysuckle picked in
the hedgerows. How much greater the pleasure may be if
the flowers themselves carry a hidden meaning. From
ancient times flowers have been symbolic. The Romans
honoured their heroes with laurel wreaths and Greek
mythology tells how many of the flowers were created. In
*Hamlet* Ophelia recites the meanings of the herbs and
flowers she carries in her arms, for William Shakespeare
was well conversant with their significance. Poets have
always extolled the virtues of flowers and since Elizabethan times have written of their meanings, but it was
the Victorians who turned flower-giving into an art.
Inspired by a book entitled *Le Langage des Fleurs* by a
French woman, Madame de la Tour, the Victorians
practised the new floral code with the same dedication
with which they built their cities and furnished their
houses. The choice of flower was all important, but so too
was the manner of presentation. If the flowers were
upside down the opposite meaning was intended, thus
tulips presented with their stems uppermost meant bla-
tant rejection from a lover. If the ribbon was tied to the

left, the meaning referred to the giver, if tied to the right, to the recipient. On the other hand she could always respond by wearing the flower in different ways – on her heart of course meant love, but worn in the hair implied caution.

From Candlemas to Christmastide our great wealth of plants can convey our sentiments without recourse to the written word. Ivy may be sent to convey fidelity and combined with a few jonquils would be the request for a *return* to faithfulness. Carnations would be sent by a heartbroken suitor but woebetide the girl who receives Narcissus – the sender will always be more interested in himself. Ardent suitors must beware when selecting their roses, for whilst the Cabbage Rose implies ambassador of love and Rose la France invites the loved one to meet by moonlight, the Yellow Rose means that love is waning.

Nobody appreciated flowers more than Elizabeth Barrett Browning, imprisoned in her sick room for long periods, and she writes with such gratitude for the posies picked for her by her husband Robert Browning. Picking flowers one has grown oneself is a great source of joy and I feel fortunate to have grown up in the country with a large garden. My father, whose passion for gardening has certainly been handed down to his children, would proudly take dinner guests to the greenhouse to show off his latest blooms. They would invariably go home with a bag of ripe tomatoes or a fine cucumber – as great a gesture of loving friendship as any of the flowers in his hothouse. I have dedicated this book to him, together with my mother and sister who have always enjoyed growing and arranging flowers, filling their homes with colour and scent, making them welcoming and very special to me.

*Sheila Pickles*
*Canonbury, 1989.*

# CONTENTS

Honeysuckle..............*Sweetness of Disposition*
Hyacinth ....................*Sorrow*
Iris..............................*Message*
Ivy .............................*Fidelity*
Jasmine......................*Grace and Elegance*
Lavender ...................*Distrust*
Lilac...........................*First Emotions of Love*
Lily..............................*Purity*
Lily of the Valley.......*Return of Happiness*
Marigold....................*Grief*
Narcissus...................*Egotism*
Nasturtium................*Patriotism*
Orchid........................*A belle*
Pansy .........................*Thoughts*
Peony.........................*Shame and Bashfulness*
Phlox..........................*Agreement*
Poppy ........................*Fantastic Extravagance*
Primrose ...................*Early Youth*
Rose ..........................*Love*
Speedwell..................*Female Fidelity*
Sunflower..................*Haughtiness*
Tulip...........................*Declaration of Love*
Violet .........................*Modesty*
Wallflower..................*Fidelity in Adversity*
Water Lily...................*Purity of Heart*

# AMARYLLIS
*Pride*

When Amaryllis fair doth show
the richness of her fiery glow,
The modest lily hides her head ;
the former seems so proudly spread
To win the gaze of human eye,
which soonest brightest things doth spy.
Yet vainly is the honour won,
since hastily her course is run ;
She blossoms, blooms, – she fades, – she dies, –
they who admired, now despise.

ANONYMOUS

HE Amaryllis is named after a shepherdess referred to in Virgil and the name comes from the Greek word meaning dazzling. The species is called *belladonna*, an Italian word meaning beautiful lady. In the Language of Flowers, the Amaryllis may be interpreted as haughty as well as proud, perhaps because the flower is difficult to grow, but once in bloom outshines all those around it. Its beauty is shortlived, however, and if we are to believe the verse, the Amaryllis leaves few friends behind.

# ANEMONE
*Forsaken*

Sweet Flower! that peeping from thy russet stem
Unfoldest timidly, (for in strange sort
This dark, frieze-coated, hoarse, teeth-chattering Month
Hath borrowed Zephyr's voice, and gazed upon thee
With blue voluptuous eye) alas, poor Flower!
*ON OBSERVING A BLOSSOM ON THE FIRST OF FEBRUARY, 1796.*
SAMUEL TAYLOR COLERIDGE, 1772-1834

THE Anemone is part of the Buttercup family but unlike its sunny cousin, is a sad little flower. Anemones have always been known as Wind-flowers, for the ancient Greeks believed they would only open their petals when the wind blew, and so named them after Anemos, the god of the wind.

Another name that country people use is Candlemas-caps, for they flower by the 2nd of February when Candlemas is celebrated in honour of the Virgin Mary.

Drops-of-snow, Granny's Nightcap and Chimney-smock are other names given to the Anemone, particularly the White Wood Anemone which grows wild in lonely woodland and whose significance is Forlornness.

Another legend tells us that when Venus was weeping in the forest for Adonis, anemones sprang up where her tears fell – perhaps why Forsaken, after all, is the true meaning.

# BLUEBELL

*Constancy*

A filbert hedge with wild briar overtwined,
And clumps of woodbine taking the soft wind
Upon their summer thrones; there too should be
The frequent chequer of a youngling tree,
That with a score of light green brethren shoots
From the quaint mossiness of aged roots:
Round which is heard a spring-head of clear waters
Babbling so wildly of its lovely daughters
The spreading blue-bells: it may haply mourn
That such fair clusters should be rudely torn
From their fresh beds, and scattered thoughtlessly
By infant hands, left on the path to die.

JOHN KEATS, 1795–1821

$\mathcal{B}$LUEBELLS are one of our hardiest wild flowers, faithfully returning year after year, and surely they mean Constancy because of their tenacity once established in a garden. They cover our woods with blue carpets each May but dislike being picked and once gathered, the nodding bells soon droop.

It is sometimes confused with the Harebell or the Bluebell of Scotland which is quite a different plant and part of the *Campanula* family. The genus name is *Endymion* and was so loved by Keats that he named the hero of his poetic romance after it.

# CAMELLIA
*Perfected Loveliness*

*Violetta.* If that is true, then leave me.
Friendship is all I can offer you.
I don't know how to love,
I couldn't feel so great an emotion.
I'm being honest with you – sincere . . .
You should look for someone else,
Then you wouldn't find it hard
To forget me. . . .

*Alfredo.* I'll do as you say. I'll go.
*(He turns away.)*

*Violetta.* So it's come to that already?
*(She takes a flower from her corsage.)*
Take this flower.

*Alfredo.* Why?

*Violetta.* So that you can bring it back to me.

*Alfredo. (turning back)* When?

*Violetta.* When it's withered.

*Alfredo.* You mean . . . tomorrow?

*Violetta.* Very well, tomorrow.

*Alfredo. (rapturously taking the flower)* I'm happy . . .
Oh, so happy!

LIBRETTO FROM *LA TRAVIATA*, GIUSEPPE VERDI, 1813–1901

THE Camellia is named after George Joseph Camellus, a Jesuit from Moravia. They are native to India, China and Japan where he travelled, and the flowers are often depicted in Oriental Art. They were featured in Alexander Dumas' book *The Lady of the Camellias* where the heroine conveyed her feelings to her suitors by wearing red or white camellias. The meaning of the White Camellia is Unpretending Excellence.

# CARNATION

*Red Carnation – Alas for my poor heart*
*Striped Carnation – Refusal*
*Yellow Carnation – Disdain*

*Perdita.* Sir, the year growing ancient,
Not yet on summer's death nor on the birth
Of trembling winter, the fairest flowers o' th'season
Are our Carnation and streak'd gillyvors
Which some call nature's bastards.
*THE WINTER'S TALE*, WILLIAM SHAKESPEARE, 1564–1616

*I*N the Language of Flowers the Carnation changes its meaning according to its colour, so whilst the Striped Carnation means Refusal and the Yellow Carnation Disdain, the Red Carnation signifies the blood of Christ.

The cultivation of these confident flowers goes back over two thousand years and it is said that the plant came to England with the Normans. It may be found growing wild in the walls of the Norman castles of Dover and Rochester and is believed to have been rooted to the stones imported from France.

The Athenians honoured Carnations by calling them Di-anthos, Flower of Jove, and used the flowers to make wreaths and garlands at their festivals, whence came the word "coronation" from which Carnation is derived. Due to their clove-like scent they are frequently referred to as gillyflowers, a name they share with both wallflowers and stocks, coming from the French "giroflier". Carnations were sometimes added to wine and ale to add spiciness and are still known as sops-in-wine in some parts of the countryside today.

# CHRYSANTHEMUM

*Red Chrysanthemum – I Love*
*Yellow Chrysanthemum – Slighted Love*
*White Chrysanthemum – Truth*

To love one maiden only, cleave to her,
And worship her by years of noble deeds,
Until they won her ; for indeed I knew
Of no more subtle master under heaven
Than is the maiden passion for a maid,
Not only to keep down the base in man,
But teach high thought, and amiable words
And courtliness, and the desire of fame,
And love of truth, and all that makes a man.
ALFRED, LORD TENNYSON, 1809–1892

*HE* Chrysanthemum must feel a poor immigrant in
the West where it is welcomed only in the autumn
because of the scarcity of other flowers. It has been grown
in the Far East for over two thousand years, and so
admired in Japan that the Emperor sits on the Chrysanthemum Throne. The name comes from the Greek words
"chrysos", meaning gold, and "anthemon", a flower, for
the species grown was a yellow one. Today their colours
include all shades of yellow, pink and rusty red, but my
favourite is the bronze, rose-madder.

The family includes the simple Daisy, the small Dwarf
Chrysanthemum, and the double-flowered Cottage Bronze
which flowers late into the autumn. Then there are the
varieties grown for cutting and arranging indoors. These
have heavy round heads and curly petals growing tightly
into a ball. It always seems a miracle of nature that such a
thin stem can support such a heavy head.

# CLEMATIS
*Mental Beauty*

A thing of beauty is a joy for ever :
Its loveliness increases ; it will never
Pass into nothingness ; but still will keep
A bower quiet for us, and a sleep
Full of sweet dreams, and health, and quiet breathing.
Therefore, on every morrow, are we wreathing
A flowery band to bind us to the earth.

*ENDYMION*, JOHN KEATS, 1795–1821

LEMATIS was named Klema by the ancient Greeks after a vine, for the Clematis entwines itself round other plants until its head is in the sunlight. Some people call it Love-bind because it clings as if in a loving embrace and in the country the Wild Clematis which scrambles over hedgerows is known as Hedgevine or Traveller's Joy.

Poets have often referred to this delicate trailing plant as Virgin's Bower for it trails prettily over arbours and shady places in the garden, thus making a pleasant refuge for young ladies. Some people think the name was in honour of Queen Elizabeth, the Virgin Queen, for it was introduced into England during her reign. Others believed that the Clematis sheltered the Virgin Mary during the flight from Egypt, with Joseph and the Christ-Child.

When the Clematis has flowered it looks like a man's beard, with whitish, feathery tufts, and has been called Old-man's-beard or Grandfather's Whiskers. The plant is also called Maiden-hair, because it resembles the finely-spun hair of a young girl. Perhaps the significance of Mental Beauty refers to the fact that the Clematis has no healing properties and is grown solely for its appearance.

# COLUMBINE
*Folly*

*Ophelia.* There's rosemary, that's for remembrance;
pray you, love, remember. And there is pansies, that's for
thoughts.

*Laertes.* A document in madness—thoughts and remembrance fitted.

*Ophelia.* There's fennel for you, and columbines.
There's rue for you; and here's some for me. We may call
it herb of grace a Sundays. O, you must wear your rue
with a difference. There's a daisy. I would give you some
violets, but they wither'd all when my father died. They
say 'a made a good end.

HAMLET, WILLIAM SHAKESPEARE, 1564–1616

*P*OOR mad Ophelia rightly carried columbines in her
arms, for Shakespeare was well versed in the Language
of Flowers and columbines were perfect for the bouquet of
a deserted lover. The red flower signifies Anxiety and the
purple, Resolution.

In the country it is known as Granny's Bonnet and the

genus name, *Aquilegia,* is from the Latin word for eagle, the base of the flower resembling an eagle's claws. It reminded others of a flight of doves for it was named Columbine from the Latin "columba" meaning dove. It is also due to this association that the flower has become a symbol of the Holy Spirit and appears often in religious paintings by the great masters.

# CORNFLOWER
*Delicacy*

So sweet love seemed that April morn,
When first we kissed beside the thorn,
So strangely sweet, it was not strange
We thought that love could never change.

But I can tell—let truth be told—
That love will change in growing old;
Though day by day is nought to see,
So delicate his motions be.
*SO SWEET LOVE SEEMED,* ROBERT BRIDGES, 1844-1930

*I*N olden days, if a girl wore a cornflower it meant she was available for marriage. If a young man put a cornflower in his pocket, he was in love. If the flower lived it was a sign that he should marry; if it died, he must find another sweetheart. It was also believed that if a girl hid the flower under her apron, she would have the bachelor of her choice. Hence the name Bachelor's Buttons.

This vivid blue flower, which grows wild in cornfields, is also known as Bluebottle, Ragged Sailor or Hurt-sickle, because its tough stems blunt the reaper's tools. Its genus name of *Centaurea* comes from the ancient Greeks. Chiron the Centaur was wounded by Hercules' poisonous arrows but covered his wounds with cornflowers and was healed. The species name, *cyanus,* is also of classical origin. Once upon a time a young boy worshipped Flora, the goddess of flowers. He was particularly fond of the blue flowers which he gathered in the cornfields near his house. One day he was found dead there and Flora turned him into a cornflower in honour of his love for the flower and his sensitivity towards her. So the significance of the Cornflower became Delicacy.

# CROWN IMPERIAL
*Majesty and Power*

... bold oxlips, and
The crown-imperial; lilies of all kinds,
The flow'r-de-luce being one. O, these I lack.
To make you garlands of and my sweet friend
To strew him o'er and o'er!

*THE WINTER'S TALE.* WILLIAM SHAKESPEARE, 1564–1616

*I*T is easy to see why the Crown Imperial is so named
for it is the most majestic of flowers. As its meaning
suggests, it grows to a great height and looks down on all
the surrounding flowers, as a king may look down on his
subjects.

Whilst the Crown Imperial came originally from
Constantinople, it was first known as the Persian Lily for
it was brought to Europe from Persia in the Sixteenth
Century. It has always been admired for its imperious
beauty but unlike most of the lily family, it has a most
unattractive scent.

# DAFFODIL
*Regard and Chivalry*

I wandered lonely as a cloud
That floats on high o'er vales and hills,
When all at once I saw a crowd,
A host of golden daffodils;
Beside the lake, beneath the trees,
Fluttering and dancing in the breeze.

Continuous as the stars that shine
And twinkle on the milky way,
They stretched in never-ending line
Along the margin of a bay:
Ten thousand saw I at a glance,
Tossing their heads in sprightly dance.

WILLIAM WORDSWORTH, 1770–1850

WORDSWORTH's famous lines have immortalised the Daffodil and there is hardly a poet in our language who has not written of it.

It is said that the name Daffodil probably comes from Affodyle, an old English word meaning early-comer. In Shakespeare's day it had many nicknames such as

daff-a-down-dilly and daffodilly and it is also known as the Lent lily. Some regard it as unlucky to have them in the house for they hang their heads and bring tears and unhappiness. This may have come from the Story of Proserpina, told by Perdita in *The Winter's Tale*, who was captured whilst picking lilies and carried off by Pluto, the Greek god. In her fear Proserpina dropped the lilies and they turned into daffodils as they touched the ground.

# DAISY

*Innocence*

I'd choose to be a daisy,
If I might be a flower;
Closing my petals softly
At twilight's quiet hour;
And waking in the morning,
When falls the early dew,
To welcome Heaven's bright sunshine,
And Heaven's bright tear-drops too.

*I'D CHOOSE TO BE A DAISY*, ANONYMOUS

THE Daisy is the children's flower. They love to gather it for posies and for making daisy chains. It is also known as Baby's-pet or Bairn-wort meaning child-flower. If a little girl picks a bunch of daisies with her eyes shut, the number of flowers in the posy will be the number of years before she marries. Young girls have always told their fortunes by pulling the petals off to the refrain "He loves me, he loves me not".

It is quite true to its name, for in the morning it opens with the light of day and when the sun goes down it folds up its white petals again as if it were going to sleep. Daisy means the day's eye, or the eye of the day.

# DANDELION
*Oracle*

Some young and saucy dandelions
Stood laughing in the sun;
They were brimming full of happiness,
And running o'er with fun.

At length they saw beside them
A dandelion old;
His form was bent and withered,
Gone were his looks of gold.

"Oh, oh!" they cried, "just see him;
"Old greybeard, how d'ye do?
We'd hide our heads in the grasses,
If we were as bald as you."

But lo! when dawned the morning,
Up rose each tiny head,
Decked not with golden tresses,
But long grey locks instead.

ANONYMOUS

THE meaning of the Dandelion is probably the one most of us learned first, for all children love to blow the seeds from the dandelion seedhead to tell the time.

They are known as Blow-balls, and Noon-head-clocks as a result and also Monk's Head and Priest's Crown, for the part of the plant that remains when all the fluffy seeds have blown away resembles the shaven head of a priest.

The name is from the French, "dent-de-lion", because the jagged edges of the leaves are like the teeth of a wild animal.

There are many superstitions about the Dandelion. A wish should come true if all the seeds are blown off in one breath; if some remain it indicates how many children you will have. Lovers use dandelion seeds to send messages to one another, for as well as divining the future, the Dandelion means Faithfulness.

# FORGET-ME-NOT
*True Love*

From off her glowing cheek, she sate and stretched
The silk upon the frame, and worked her name
Between the Moss-rose and Forget-me-not—
Her own dear name, with her own auburn hair!
That forced to wander till sweet spring return,
I yet might ne'er forget her smile, her look,
Her voice, (that even in her mirthful mood
Has made me wish to steal away and weep.)
Nor yet the entrancement of that maiden kiss
With which she promised, that when spring returned,
She would resign one half of that dear name
And own thenceforth no other name but mine!

*THE KEEP-SAKE*, SAMUEL TAYLOR COLERIDGE, 1772–1834

THE flower is associated with loving remembrance and true love. Once upon a time a knight in armour was walking along the bank of a river with his lady. She saw some flowers growing at the edge of the water and asked him to pick them for her. As the knight stretched out his hand for them, he slipped and fell into the river. Wearing heavy armour, he was unable to swim and was carried away down stream but not before he had thrown the flowers onto the bank for her. Forget-me-not! he cried as he drifted away. The maiden never forgot him and called the flower Forget-me-not in his memory.

The Forget-me-not gets its botanical name *Myosotis scorpioides* from the idea that the leaves resemble the ears of mice; all the plants of this family are known as Scorpion Grass because their clusters of flowers curl upwards like the tail of a scorpion.

# FOXGLOVE

*Insincerity*

The foxglove bells, with lolling tongue,
Will not reveal what peals were rung
In Faery, in Faery,
A thousand ages gone.
All the golden clappers hang
As if but now the changes rang;
Only from the mottled throat
Never any echoes float.
Quite forgotten, in the wood,
Pale, crowded steeples rise;
MARY WEBB

FOXGLOVES are thought of as the fairies' flower and their name is a corruption of Folk's-glove. They obviously provided more than gloves for the little folk for they are also known as Fairies'-petticoats, Fairy-caps and Fairies'-dresses. Nor was this association confined to their clothing, for other names include Fairy-thimbles and Fairy-bells. If you see a foxglove bending over, it is because the fairies are hiding in the bells.

Their genus name, *Digitalis*, means a finger-length and children have always delighted in poking their fingers into the speckled purple blooms.

But there is a darker side to the Foxglove which explains its meaning. Whilst for centuries it has been widely used as a herbal cure, excessive doses are poisonous. In Scotland they are called Bloody Fingers and Dead Men's Bells and to hear them ring forebodes an early death.

# GENTIAN
*You are unjust*

The rain it raineth on the just
And also on the unjust fella :
But chiefly on the just, because
The unjust steals the just's umbrella.

CHARLES, BARON BOWEN, 1835–1894

THIS bright blue flower is named after Gentius, King of Illyria, who was said to be an alcoholic and used the Gentian for medicinal purposes. It has remarkable healing properties and is said to be resistant to disease. It was even used by Pythagorus in the Sixth Century BC in a recipe he created as an antidote to poison. More recently Gentian has also been enjoyed as a wine.

The flowers are trumpet shaped and easy to grow, but can be temperamental, for a clump which flowers well one year may never flower again. Whilst the origin of its meaning is not known perhaps it was so called by a disappointed gardener.

# GERANIUM

*Dark Geranium – Melancholy*
*Oak-leaved Geranium – True Friendship*
*Rose or Pink Geranium – Preference*
*Scarlet Geranium – Comforting*

Beautiful Evelyn Hope is dead !
Sit and watch by her side an hour.
That is her book-shelf, this her bed ;
She plucked that piece of geranium-flower,
Beginning to die too, in the glass ;
Little has yet been changed, I think :
The shutters are shut, no light may pass
Save two long rays thro' the hinge's chink.

But the time will come,—at last it will,
When, Evelyn Hope, what meant ( I shall say )
In the lower earth, in the years long still,
That body and soul so pure and gay ?
Why your hair was amber, I shall divine,
And your mouth of your own geranium's red—
And what you would do with me, in fine,
In the new life come in the old one's stead.

ROBERT BROWNING, 1812–1889

ERANIUMS are to be found in most parts of the world and almost everywhere are confused with Pelargoniums. Their botanical name comes from the Greek word "geranos", meaning a crane, for the fruit of the plant resembles a crane's beak, hence the nickname Cranesbill. Geraniums are said to have been given their colour by Mohammed who left his clothes to dry on a bed of mallow. The flowers blushed dark red with pride and never lost their colour, and have been known as geraniums ever since. I always associate them with the Mediterranean where they tumble out of terracotta pots and down painted stone walls, the very colour of them creating a festive mood.

# HOLLYHOCK
*Female Ambition*

*Lady Macbeth*
Glamis thou art, and Cawdor; and shalt be
What thou art promis'd. Yet do I fear thy nature;
It is too full o' th' milk of human kindness
To catch the nearest way. Thou wouldst be great;
Art not without ambition, but without
The illness should attend it. What thou wouldst highly,
That wouldst thou holily; wouldst not play false,
And yet wouldst wrongly win.
MACBETH, WILLIAM SHAKESPEARE, 1564–1616

WE think of the Hollyhock as the most English of
plants, but it was imported from its native China in
the Sixteenth Century. The Chinese consider it the symbol
of fruitfulness, hence its meaning.

It quickly became popular in England, being easy to
grow, and since the leaves were used to cure horses'
swollen heels it was initially known as Hockleaf. People
wrongly attributed its origin to the Holy Land so it came
to be known as the Hollyhock. I cannot imagine a more
appropriate plant to symbolise female ambition, its tall,
pretty pastel blooms swaying at the back of our cottage
gardens.

# HONEYSUCKLE
*Sweetness of Disposition*

Ye have been fresh and green,
Ye have been fill'd with flowers :
And ye the Walks have been
Where Maids have spent their houres.

Y'ave heard them sweetly sing,
And seen them in a Round :
Each Virgin, like a Spring,
With Hony-succles crown'd.

But now, we see, none here,
Whose silv'rie feet did tread,
And with dishevell'd Haire,
Adorn'd this smoother Mead.

Like Unthrifts, having spent,
Your stock, and needy grown,
Y'are left here to lament
Your poore estates, alone.

ROBERT HERRICK, 1591–1674

*Y*ou have only to suck the honey out of the centre of the flower to see where the Honeysuckle got its name and meaning. Very sweetly scented, it is beloved by poets for its virtues and mentioned frequently by Shakespeare who often called it by the country name of Woodbine. Its woody stems twine clockwise around anything in its path, and true to its herbal name, *Caprifolium*, the flower climbs as nimbly as a goat.

Often growing in the wild, it transforms its surroundings into a place of floral enchantment by its evocative scent.

# HYACINTH
*Sorrow*

Yet art thou not inglorious in thy fate;
For so Apollo, with unweeting hand
Whilome did slay his dearly-loved mate
Young Hyacinth born on Eurotas' strand,
Young Hyacinth the pride of Spartan land;
But then transform'd him to a purple flower
Alack that so to change thee winter had no power.

JOHN MILTON, 1608–1674

In Greek mythology there was a handsome boy from Sparta called Hyacinthus. He was a great friend of Apollo, the sun god, who would descend to the earth from his golden chariot in the sky to play with him. One day the two friends were competing to see who could throw the discus the furthest. They were watched by Zephyrus, the god of the wind. He was jealous of Apollo, for he was fond of Hyacinthus and he plotted his revenge. Next time Apollo threw the heavy circular disc, Zephyrus blew the West Wind causing the disc to go off course and strike Hyacinthus a fatal blow on the head. Apollo was filled with grief at the death of his friend and created hyacinths out of the blood which had been shed. Thus Apollo ensured that the memory of his friend would live on.

# IRIS

*Message*

Thou art the Iris, fair among the fairest,
Who, armed with golden rod
And winged with the celestial azure, bearest
The message of some God.

Thou art the Muse, who far from crowded cities
Hauntest the sylvan streams,
Playing on pipes of reed the artless ditties
That come to us as dreams.

O flower-de-luce, bloom on, and let the river
Linger to kiss thy feet!
O flower of song, bloom on, and make for ever
The world more fair and sweet.

HENRY WADSWORTH LONGFELLOW, 1807–1882

*I*RIS was the messenger of the ancient Greek gods and
she appeared to the mortals on earth in the form of a
rainbow. The glorious arc was said to be the flight of Iris
winging a message across the sky. She was as fleet of foot
as the bloom of the flower is short, and there are as many
different shades of the Iris as there are colours of the
rainbow.

The Iris had many admirers, including the kings of
France who used it as their royal emblem, and called it the
Fleur-de-Lis. Shakespeare often referred to the flower in
his plays by the anglicised name Flower-de-Luce.

T.N. JACKSON 1894.

# IVY
*Fidelity*

With honeysuckle, over-sweet, festooned;
With bitter ivy bound;
Terraced with funguses unsound;
Deformed with many a boss
And closèd scar, o'ercushioned deep with moss;
Bunched all about with pagan mistletoe;
And thick with nests of the hoarse bird
That talks, but understands not his own word;
Stands, and so stood a thousand years ago,
A single tree.
COVENTRY PATMORE. 1823–1896

THE Ivy is not able to support itself but depends upon trees and walls up which to climb. But once it has gained hold, nothing can separate it, hence its meaning. It does not live off its partner, however, but feeds off its own roots.

We associate it in our minds with Holly for they are both used to decorate our houses at Christmas. This

tradition originated centuries ago in order to protect us
from evil spirits: the druids believed the Holly and the
Ivy had magical properties and would drive away the
devil. It was even hung in the cow-shed to stop the milk
from turning sour.

If it grew on the wall of a house the occupants would be
safe from witches and if it died, disaster was anticipated.
In Wales, if the ivy failed, it meant that the house would
pass into other hands, probably through infertility. Ivy,
with its clinging habit, is a feminine symbol. Girls living
in Oxfordshire learned to put an ivy leaf in their pocket
before strolling out. Then the first man they encountered
was their bridegroom to be.

# JASMINE

*Yellow Jasmine – Grace and Elegance*
*White Jasmine – Amiability*
*Spanish Jasmine – Sensuality*

My pensive Sara! thy soft cheek reclined
Thus on mine arm, most soothing sweet it is
To sit beside our cot, our cot o'ergrown
With white-flowered Jasmin, and the broad-leaved Myrtle,
(Meet emblems they of Innocence and Love!)
*THE ÆOLIAN HARP.* SAMUEL TAYLOR COLERIDGE. 1772–1834

THE name comes from the Arabic, "jas" meaning despair and "min" meaning a lie. It is as famous for its scent as its flower, having an exotic, heady perfume which is especially intoxicating at night. The Hindus gave it the beautiful name Moonlight of the Grove.

# LAVENDER
*Distrust*

And still she slept an azure-lidded sleep,
In blanched linen, smooth, and lavender'd,
While he from forth the closet brought a heap
Of candied apple, quince, and plum, and gourd;
With jellies soother than the creamy curd,
And lucent syrops, tinct with cinnamon;
Manna and dates, in argosy transferr'd
From Fez; and spiced dainties, every one,
From silken Samarcand to cedar'd Lebanon.

THE EVE OF ST. AGNES, JOHN KEATS, 1795–1821

FOR centuries Lavender has been used in the home to
scent linen chests, perfume soap and eau de Cologne,
and as a herbal cure. The Elizabethans scattered it on the
floor to scent their houses and to deter moths and insects.

According to folklore, small poisonous snakes known as
asps like to lie under lavender bushes. So people grew to
distrust the plant, and the language of Lavender came to
express exactly that sentiment.

# LILAC
*First Emotions of Love*

O were my Love yon lilac fair,
Wi' purple blossoms to the spring,
And I a bird to shelter there,
When wearied on my little wing;
How I wad mourn when it was torn
By autumn wild and winter rude!
But I wad sing on wanton wing
When youthfu' May its bloom renew'd.

ROBERT BURNS, 1759–1796

HE Lilac is a member of the olive family but it used to be known as Blue-pipe in allusion to the hollow stems which were used for pipes. The name comes from the Greek word "syringa" meaning tube and it is probable that the plant originated in Greece or Southern Europe. But it has become a great favourite in England and has been widely planted here since the time of Henry VIII.

Country people call it May Flower and Lily-oak and many are superstitious about bringing it indoors, particularly the white variety whose meaning is Youthful Innocence. Like many white flowers it is also associated with death and indeed it refuses to bloom if another lilac is cut down in the garden.

It is curious that in the Language of Flowers the Lilac should symbolise such pure sentiments for in some villages a lilac branch is said to signify a broken engagement.

# LILY
*Purity*

And the stately lilies stand
Fair in silvery light
Like saintly vestals, pale in prayer;
Their pure breath sanctifies the air,
As its fragrance fills the night.
ANONYMOUS

THE Lily has always been regarded as the symbol of purity and is one of the oldest flowers in the world. It may be found painted on the walls of ancient Greek palaces where it was the personal flower of Hera, the moon goddess.

The Lily is dedicated to the Virgin Mary in honour of her purity which is perhaps why many brides like to include it in their bouquets, and why it may be found at many religious festivals. Legend has it that the first lily sprang up from the tears dropped by Eve when she left the Garden of Eden.

# LILY OF THE VALLEY
*Return of Happiness*

My heart aches, and a drowsy numbness pains
My sense, as though of hemlock I had drunk,
Or emptied some dull opiate to the drains
One minute past, and Lethe-wards had sunk :
    'Tis not through envy of thy happy lot,
    But being too happy in thine happiness,—
That thou, light-winged Dryad of the trees,
        In some melodious plot
Of beechen green, and shadows numberless,
Singest of summer in full-throated ease.
*ODE TO A NIGHTINGALE*, JOHN KEATS, 1795-1821

$\mathscr{I}$T is not surprising that the Lily of the Valley symbolises the Return of Happiness for it is the sweetest flower imaginable. With its dainty white bells and unmistakable green scent it is said to lure the nightingale from his nest and lead him to his mate.

It is the symbol of May Day and was known as May Lily and Our Lady's Tears because it grew from the tears shed by the Virgin Mary at the Cross. The flowers were grown by monks for decorating the altar and were called Ladder to Heaven because the miniature flower-bells grow like steps up the stem.

# MARIGOLD

*Grief*

Open afresh your round of starry folds,
Ye ardent marigolds!
Dry up the moisture from your golden lids,
For great Apollo bids
That in these days your praises should be sung
On many harps, which he has lately strung;
And when again your dewiness he kisses,
Tell him, I have you in my world of blisses:
So haply when I rove in some far vale,
His mighty voice may come upon the gale.

JOHN KEATS, 1795–1821

THE Marigold, *Calendula*, has always been associated with the sun's journey across the sky, from nine in the morning until three in the afternoon. The Victorians believed they could set the clock by the hour the Marigold opened and closed its colourful petals. *Calendula* is the name of the genus because it flowers all round the calendar year, and the name Marigold probably means Mary-gold after the Virgin Mary. In some parts they are also known as Mary-bud and Mary-gold. Lots of children have been reminded of a button when looking at the big, round flower, and so have called them Bachelor's Buttons, a name they share with several other members of the daisy family.

The Marigold signifies Grief, it is believed, because the flower daily mourns the departure of the sun when its petals are forced to close.

# NARCISSUS

*Egotism*

What first inspired a bard of old to sing
Narcissus pining o'er the untainted spring?
In some delicious ramble, he had found
A little space, with boughs all woven round;
And in the midst of all, a clearer pool
Than e'er reflected in its pleasant cool,
The blue sky here, and there, serenely peeping
Through tendril wreaths fantastically creeping.
And on the bank a lonely flower he spied,
A meek and forlorn flower, with naught of pride,
Drooping its beauty o'er the watery clearness,
To woo its own sad image into nearness:
Deaf to light Zephyrus it would not move;
But still would seem to droop, to pine, to love.
So while the poet stood in this sweet spot,
Some fainter gleamings o'er his fancy shot;
Nor was it long ere he had told the tale
Of young Narcissus, and sad Echo's bale.

JOHN KEATS. 1795–1821

*I*n classical mythology there was a beautiful Greek shepherd boy named Narcissus. He was loved by all the wood nymphs, but one in particular had lost her heart to him. This was Echo. She was unable to tell him of her love for she could only repeat his last words. He was quite unaware of her adoration, which he did not reciprocate, and did not even realise that he was the cause of her unhappiness. In time she became so pale and thin that she looked like nothing but a little gossamer spirit following him through the trees, and at last she wandered off to the mountains where she pined away until she became nothing but a voice.

Meanwhile, Venus, the goddess of love, heard of Echo's hopeless devotion and determined to punish the hard-hearted boy. When Narcissus was hunting in the forest she arranged for Cupid to set a magic spell upon him. Coming to a clear pool he stopped to quench his thirst and there in the water he saw another face rise up to meet his own as he leant over. For the first time in his life, Narcissus fell in love. He plunged his arms into the water without success to catch the lovely spirit who dwelt there. He sang out to the beautiful creature but the only answer was the faint, sad echo from the distant mountains.

Poor Narcissus! How could he know that all the time he was looking at his own reflection. He had fallen hopelessly in love with his own beautiful face mirrored in the pool. Day after day he returned, his tears falling into the pool like rain, until finally he began to pine and fade just as Echo had done in her turn, with the sad hopelessness of unrequited love. Then the Immortals took pity on him, and turned him into a delicate white papery flower which grows forever by the pool, in memory of the egotistical youth.

# NASTURTIUM
*Patriotism*

If I should die, think only this of me :
That there's some corner of a foreign field
That is for ever England. There shall be
In that rich earth a richer dust concealed ;
A dust whom England bore, shaped, made aware,
Gave, once, her flowers to love, her ways to roam,
A body of England's, breathing English air,
Washed by the rivers, blest by suns of home.
*THE SOLDIER,* RUPERT BROOKE, 1887–1915

THE significance of the Nasturtium in the Language of Flowers is probably due to the fact that it came to England from the New World in the Sixteenth Century, at the same time as tobacco. It was then banished to the kitchen garden and grown for centuries as a salad. Its name, Nasturtium, which it shares with watercress, comes from the Latin phrase for "twisted nose" and it refers to the peppery taste they have in common. Its botanical name comes from the Greek word meaning trophy because the flowers and leaves are shaped like helmets and shields – perhaps another explanation for its symbolism.

# ORCHID
## *A belle*

I met a lady in the meads
Full beautiful, a faery's child;
Her hair was long, her foot was light,
And her eyes were wild.

I set her on my pacing steed,
And nothing else saw all day long;
For sideways would she lean, and sing
A faery's song.

I made a garland for her head,
And bracelets too, and fragrant zone;
She look'd at me as she did love,
And made sweet moan.

She found me roots of relish sweet,
And honey wild, and manna dew;
And sure in language strange she said,
I love thee true.

*LA BELLE DAME SANS MERCI*, JOHN KEATS, 1795-1821

WE think of orchids as exotic flowers, the product of hothouses and warm climes, but there are a lot of smaller orchids which grow wild in English fields and hedgerows. All orchids have spots, their very own beauty marks, and folklore tells us that there were orchids growing at the foot of the Cross when Jesus was crucified. His blood dropped on the flowers and they have carried the stain ever since.

As different species have varying blooms of curious shapes, so the Orchid has been named Adder's-tongue, Dead Men's Fingers, Ram's-horns and variously after Mother Goose and her goslings, Giddy-gander and Goosie-gander, on account of the way the flowers are grouped on the stem. Orchids are highly prized and quite unique, as their language implies.

# PANSY
*Thoughts*

I send thee pansies while the year is young,
Yellow as sunshine, purple as the night;
Flowers of remembrance, ever fondly sung
By all the chiefest of the sons of light;
And if in recollection lives regret
For wasted days, and dreams that were not true,
I tell thee that the pansy "freaked with jet"
Is still the heart's-ease that the poets knew.
Take all the sweetness of a gift unsought,
And for the pansies send me back a thought.

SARAH DOUDNEY

*P*ANSY is just an English way of saying the French word "pensée" which means thought, and people used to send these flowers for their nearest and dearest to remember them by. The small velvet plants we grow in our summer borders were first bred in Victorian times from the Wild Pansy which Shakespeare described as Love-in-idleness. This little flower with the smiling face was said to be a love potion, and was the cause of Titania falling in love with an ass in *A Midsummer Night's Dream*.

Wild Pansy has always been a favourite with children and country folk who have given it many affectionate names – Two-faces-under-the-sun, Face-and-hood and Tickle-my-fancy. It has also been called Herb Trinity, because there are often three colours in the one flower, reminding us of the Holy Trinity. Perhaps the best known of all the names, however, is Heartsease, for it was believed that by carrying the flower about with you, you would ensure the love of your sweetheart.

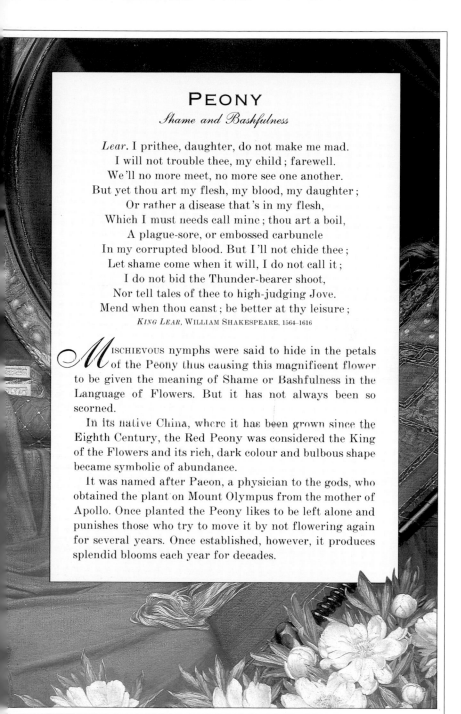

# PEONY
*Shame and Bashfulness*

*Lear.* I prithee, daughter, do not make me mad.
I will not trouble thee, my child; farewell.
We'll no more meet, no more see one another.
But yet thou art my flesh, my blood, my daughter;
Or rather a disease that's in my flesh,
Which I must needs call mine; thou art a boil,
A plague-sore, or embossed carbuncle
In my corrupted blood. But I'll not chide thee;
Let shame come when it will, I do not call it;
I do not bid the Thunder-bearer shoot,
Nor tell tales of thee to high-judging Jove.
Mend when thou canst; be better at thy leisure;

*KING LEAR*, WILLIAM SHAKESPEARE, 1564–1616

ISCHIEVOUS nymphs were said to hide in the petals
of the Peony thus causing this magnificent flower
to be given the meaning of Shame or Bashfulness in the
Language of Flowers. But it has not always been so
scorned.

In its native China, where it has been grown since the
Eighth Century, the Red Peony was considered the King
of the Flowers and its rich, dark colour and bulbous shape
became symbolic of abundance.

It was named after Paeon, a physician to the gods, who
obtained the plant on Mount Olympus from the mother of
Apollo. Once planted the Peony likes to be left alone and
punishes those who try to move it by not flowering again
for several years. Once established, however, it produces
splendid blooms each year for decades.

# PHLOX

*Agreement*

My true love hath my heart and I have his,
By just exchange one for another geven :
I holde his deare, and mine he cannot misse,
There never was a better bargaine driven.
My true love hath my heart and I have his.
My heart in me keepes him and me in one,
My heart in him his thoughts and sences guides :
He loves my heart, for once it was his owne,
I cherish his because in me it bides.
My true love hath my heart, and I have his.

*JUST EXCHANGE*, Sir Philip Sidney, 1554-1586

*D*IFFERENT interpretations have been given to the language of Phlox but the message it most commonly conveys is one of Agreement. Perhaps more ardent suitors were intoxicated by its heady scent, which perfumes the whole garden in the early evening, and felt inspired to a proposal of love. It was named after the Greek word "phlox" meaning flame, no doubt referring to their colour and shape. Beloved by cottagers for their fiery clusters of flowers, they are equally at home in the grandest herbaceous borders and are to be found in some of the finest gardens in the land.

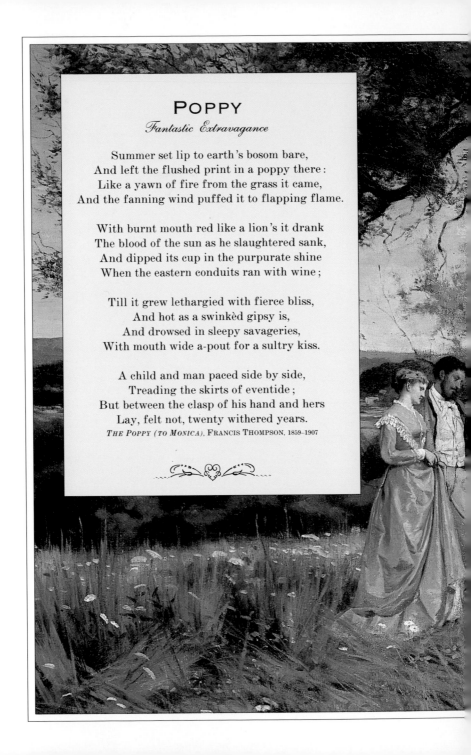

# POPPY
*Fantastic Extravagance*

Summer set lip to earth's bosom bare,
And left the flushed print in a poppy there :
Like a yawn of fire from the grass it came,
And the fanning wind puffed it to flapping flame.

With burnt mouth red like a lion's it drank
The blood of the sun as he slaughtered sank,
And dipped its cup in the purpurate shine
When the eastern conduits ran with wine ;

Till it grew lethargied with fierce bliss,
And hot as a swinkèd gipsy is,
And drowsed in sleepy savageries,
With mouth wide a-pout for a sultry kiss.

A child and man paced side by side,
Treading the skirts of eventide ;
But between the clasp of his hand and hers
Lay, felt not, twenty withered years.

*THE POPPY (TO MONICA)*, FRANCIS THOMPSON, 1859–1907

*I*N the Language of Flowers the Scarlet Poppy means Fantastic Extravagance; the White Opium Poppy from Asia means Sleep. Some people think that its Latin name, *Papaver* came from "pap" because the juice was given to babies in their food to make them sleepy.

The Poppy is sometimes called the Red Rose of Ceres for the ancient Romans believed that the flower was raised by Ceres, the corn goddess, who is always depicted carrying poppies and corn, and who offered them as a sacrifice to the gods.

One of the old country names for the Poppy was Cheesebowl for there is a little round bowl in the bottom of the flower-head filled with seeds set in something which resembles cheese. In the North of England they call it Cock-rose, Cup Rose or Corn Rose, while some call them Soldiers because of the scarlet tunics once worn as army uniform. This is ironic because they will always be associated with the Great War, springing up to cover the corpses of those who fought bravely on the battlefields of Northern France.

Many children are afraid to pick poppies because they believe that the petals will fall (as they always do) and they will be struck by thunder. So they call them Thunder Flowers.

The other name which is given to poppies all over the country is Headaches, because it is said that the smell, or the vivid colour, is bound to induce a pain in the head.

# PRIMROSE
*Early Youth*

*Perdita.* Now, my fair'st friend,
I would I had some flow'rs o' th' spring that might
Become your time of day—and yours, and yours,
That wear upon your virgin branches yet
Your maidenheads growing. O Proserpina,
For the flowers now that, frighted, thou let'st fall
From Dis's waggon! . . .
. . . pale primroses,
That die unmarried ere they can behold
Bright Phœbus in his strength—a malady
Most incident to maids
*THE WINTER'S TALE,* WILLIAM SHAKESPEARE, 1564–1616

*T*HERE are few flowers whose coming is so eagerly
awaited in the year as the Primrose and it is because it
is one of the early signs of spring that it received its name
which means "first rose". It is not what we would call a
rose today, but long ago the name was used more widely.
In parts of western England the Primrose is still called
the Butter-rose, because the colour of the flowers is so like
that of the farmhouse butter which is made there.

Primroses became very fashionable in Victorian times
and were Disraeli's favourite flower. Queen Victoria sent
him many bunches from her gardens during her reign,
and on his death she sent a large wreath of Primroses as a
token of her affection and respect.

# ROSE

*Rose – Love*
*White Rose – Purity and Spiritual Love*
*Yellow Rose – Decrease of Love and Infidelity*
*Cabbage Rose – Ambassador of Love*
*Musk Rose – Capricious Beauty*
*Single Rose – Simplicity*

If Jove would give the leafy bowers
A queen for all their world of flowers,
The rose would be the choice of Jove,
And blush the queen of every grove.
Sweetest child of weeping morning,
Gem, the breast of earth adorning,
Eye of flow'rets, glow of lawns,
Bud of beauty, nursed by dawns:
Soft the soul of love it breathes,
Cypria's brow with magic wreathes;
And to Zephyr's wild caresses,
Diffuses all its verdant tresses,
Till glowing with the wanton's play,
It blushes a diviner ray.

SAPPHO OF LESBOS. c. 600 BC.

THE Rose is one of the oldest flowers known to man, and still one of the most popular. Nebuchadnezzar used them to adorn his palace and in Persia, where they were grown for their perfume oil, the petals were used to fill the Sultan's mattress. In Kashmir the Moghul emperors cultivated beautiful rose gardens and roses were strewn in the river to welcome them on their return home. Roses later became synonymous with the worst excesses of the Roman empire – the peasants were reduced to growing roses instead of food crops in order to satisfy the demands of their rulers. The emperors filled their swimming baths and fountains with rose-water and sat on carpets of rose petals for their feasts and orgies. Heliogabalus used to enjoy showering his guests with rose petals which tumbled down from the ceiling during the festivities.

The Rose is the flower of love. It was created by Chloris, the Greek goddess of flowers, out of the lifeless body of a nymph which she found one day in a clearing in the woods. She asked the help of Aphrodite, the goddess of love, who gave her beauty; Dionysus, the god of wine, added nectar to give her a sweet scent, and the three Graces gave her charm, brightness and joy. Then Zephyr, the West Wind, blew away the clouds so that Apollo, the sun god, could shine and make the flower bloom. And so the Rose was born and was immediately crowned Queen of the Flowers.

*T*HERE are many legends telling how red roses got their colour. The Romans believed that Venus blushed when Jupiter caught her bathing and the white rose turned red in her reflection. The Greek legend tells how Aphrodite and Persephone were both in love with Adonis and used to share his favours. However, when Aphrodite decided to prevent Adonis from returning to her rival in the underworld, Persephone asked Ares, the god of war, to help her. When Adonis was hunting in the woods one day, he was fatally attacked by a wild boar. Aphrodite flew to his side, scratching herself on a white rose bush in her haste. Red roses sprang up where Adonis' blood had spilled and the white roses of the bush turned red in sympathy.

The early Christians made red roses the symbol for martyr's blood and white roses have always been associated with innocence and purity. The Virgin Mary is said to have put her veil to dry on a red rose bush which thereafter produced pure white flowers. Red and white roses together mean unity in the Language of Flowers. In the Wars of the Roses, the white rose was the emblem of the House of York and the red rose, that of the House of Lancaster. Shakespeare dramatised the scene in *Henry VI*, when each side plucked the roses in the Temple garden in London. After over thirty years of civil war the two houses were finally united by marriage and the two roses were joined to form the symbolic Tudor Rose which still appears in our heraldry today. A red and white damask rose has since been bred and named the York and Lancaster Rose.

The meaning of the Yellow Rose in the Language of Flowers is Decrease of Love and Infidelity. This may be traced back to Aisha, the favourite wife of the prophet Mohammed. He suspected her of unfaithfulness and asked the advice of the archangel Gabriel. On his return Aisha greeted him with some red roses and on the instructions of the archangel he ordered her to drop them in the river, knowing that if they changed colour his suspicions were confirmed. The roses turned yellow.

$\mathcal{Q}$UEEN Elizabeth I, known as the Virgin Queen, took the Tudor Rose as her emblem and chose "Rosa sine spina" as her motto. She was known as the rose without a thorn and many of the Elizabethan poets wrote of her.

The Rose has been the national emblem of England ever since. As a nation we are famous for our roses and there is hardly a garden in the land without them. There is nothing to equal their scent and we are fortunate that the perfumers' art is so sophisticated that they are able to reproduce the perfume for ourselves and our homes. But it is Shakespeare who so perfectly summarises the virtues of the rose in his sonnet.

O, how much more doth beauty beauteous seem
By that sweet ornament which truth doth give!
The rose looks fair, but fairer we it deem
For that sweet odour which doth in it live.
The canker-blooms have full as deep a dye,
As the perfumed tincture of the roses,
Hang on such thorns, and play as wantonly
When summer's breath their masked buds discloses:
But for their virtue only is their show,
They lived unwoo'd, and unrespected fade,
Die to themselves. Sweet roses do not so;
Of their sweet deaths are sweetest odours made.
And so of you, beauteous and lovely youth,
When that shall fade, my verse distills your truth.

*SONNET LIV.* WILLIAM SHAKESPEARE. 1564–1616

Gather ye rosebuds while ye may,
Old Time is still a-flying:
And this same flower that smiles to-day,
To-morrow will be dying.

ROBERT HERRICK, 1591-1674

# SPEEDWELL
*Female Fidelity*

Beloved, it is morn!
A redder berry on the thorn,
A deeper yellow on the corn,
For this good day new-born:
Pray, Sweet, for me
That I may be
Faithful to God and thee.

EMILY HENRIETTA HICKEY, 1845-1924

SPEEDWELL grows wild on banks and hedgerows and covers the ground in the spring with its brilliant blue flowers. Its appearance has caused the little plant to be called by many "eye" names, after the sharp little eyes of a bird, or the little eye which looks out at you from the heart of the flower. It is commonly known as Bird's-eye, but also Angels'-eyes, Cats'-eyes, Bright-eye and Milkmaid's-eye.

The genus name is *Veronica*, the origin of which is uncertain. It seems possible that it comes from the Greek word "beronike" meaning a faithful likeness. More likely the plant is called Speedwell because the flowers fall as soon as it is picked and people fancied it was like saying goodbye to a parting friend.

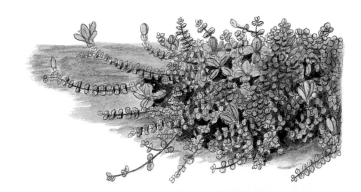

# SUNFLOWER
### *Haughtiness*

No, the heart that has truly lov'd never forgets,
But as truly loves on to the close,
As the sun-flower turns on her god, when he sets,
The same look which she turn'd when he rose.
THOMAS MOORE, 1779-1852

THE Sunflower surely has a right to feel haughty for it is by far the tallest plant in the garden. Its size is not its only asset, however, for every part of the plant is used in some way: the seeds for eating and making oil and soap; the leaves and stalks for fodder and making cloth and even as a substitute for tobacco.

The genus name of *Helianthus* comes from two Greek words, "helios" meaning sun and "anthos" meaning flower. It was worshipped as the symbol of the sun by the Incas of Peru and later by the North American Indians. There is a classical legend that Clytie, a water nymph, was changed into a sunflower having died of a broken heart at the betrayal of Apollo, the sun god.

Other names include the Marigold of Peru and the Indian Sun, but my favourite is the Italian name "Girasole" because the flowers really do turn their heads to follow the sun's daily course from east to west.

# TULIP

*Red Tulip – Declaration of Love*
*Variegated Tulip – Beautiful Eyes*
*Yellow Tulip – Hopeless Love*

But love, first learned in a lady's eyes,
Lives not alone immured in the brain,
But, with the motion of all elements,
Courses as swift as thought in every power,
And gives to every power a double power,
Above their functions and their offices.
It adds a precious seeing to the eye;
A lover's eyes will gaze an eagle blind;
A lover's ears will hear the lowest sound,
When the suspicious head of theft is stopp'd:
Love's feeling is more soft and sensible
Than are the tender horns of cockled snails:
Love's tongue proves dainty Bacchus gross in taste.
For valour, is not love a Hercules,
Still climbing trees in the Hesperides?
Subtle as Sphinx; as sweet and musical
As bright Apollo's lute, strung with his hair;
And when Love speaks, the voice of all the gods
Makes heaven drowsy with the harmony.
Never durst poet touch a pen to write
Until his ink were temper'd with Love's sighs.

LOVE'S LABOUR'S LOST, WILLIAM SHAKESPEARE, 1564-1616

*N*o flower has gone in and out of vogue quite so much as the Tulip. Condemned for many years in England to town parks and railway station gardens, they are now once again appreciated for their glorious colours and party-frock petals. Cultivated and prized like jewels by the Turks and highly regarded also by the Persians, their name comes from the Persian word "tulipant" meaning turban which was used to describe the shape of the flower. They were introduced into European gardens in the Sixteenth Century and were generally welcomed, but it

was Holland that took the flower to its heart, and its pocket, and the cultivation and buying and selling of bulbs reached such a frenzy that the economy of the country was put in jeopardy. Several decades later the hysteria hit England where the government was forced to pass a law limiting the price of a single bulb to four hundred old English pounds.

Tulips are grown solely for pleasure, having no value for the herbalist. They did finally make themselves useful, however, when the hungry peoples of occupied Europe were reduced to eating them during the war.

# VIOLET
*Modesty*

For Hamlet, and the trifling of his favour
Hold it a fashion, and a toy in blood;
A violet in the youth of primary nature
Forward, not permanent, sweet, not lasting,
The perfume and suppliance of a minute;
No more.

HAMLET, WILLIAM SHAKESPEARE, 1564–1616

THIS humble flower has been celebrated in poetry and romance from ancient times and is much loved for its delicate powdery scent. It was widely referred to by Shakespeare, who called it "forward", for it blooms early and heralds the approach of summer. The plant is often described as modest for hiding its dark beauty away in the long grass and for flowering so fleetingly.

There are many stories regarding the Violet's name, but it almost certainly originated in Greece where it was considered the flower of Zeus, the king of the gods. Legend has it that Zeus was in love with a beautiful maiden called Io and in order to protect her from Hera, his jealous wife, he changed her into a beautiful calf. Then in order to feed her with delicacies, he commanded the earth to bring forth a beautiful flower in her honour, which he named Ion, the Greek word for Viola.

# WALLFLOWER
*Fidelity in Adversity*

Heard melodies are sweet, but those unheard
Are sweeter; therefore, ye soft pipes, play on;
Not to the sensual ear, but, more endear'd,
Pipe to the spirit ditties of no tone:
Fair youth, beneath the trees, thou canst not leave
Thy song, nor ever can those trees be bare;
Bold Lover, never, never canst thou kiss,
Though winning near the goal—yet, do not grieve;
She cannot fade, though thou hast not thy bliss,
For ever wilt thou love, and she be fair!

*ODE ON A GRECIAN URN*, JOHN KEATS, 1795-1821

WALLFLOWERS are so popular because they bloom at exactly that time in the garden's calendar when the spring flowers are over and the summer border is still bare. Their name, *Cheiranthus*, comes from the Greek words meaning hand and flowers, for bouquets of wall flower were carried during ancient feasts and festivals.

The story of the origin of the meaning of Wallflower is a sad one. A Scottish nobleman's daughter was engaged to be married to a prince, but her true love was a chieftain. He disguised himself as a minstrel and sang underneath the tower where her father had imprisoned her. She threw him a wallflower and then attempted to climb down the walls of the castle to join her love. But the ladder broke and she fell to her death beside the flower. He declared that he would remain faithful to her memory and the Wallflower became his emblem. A perfect symbol for Fidelity in Adversity.

# WATER LILY
*Purity of Heart*

Now folds the lily all her sweetness up,
And slips into the bosom of the lake :
So fold thyself, my dearest, thou, and slip
Into my bosom and be lost in me.
ALFRED, LORD TENNYSON, 1809–1892

WATER Lilies take their name from the
Greek water nymph, Nymphe, the goddess
of springs, as they were found growing where
the nymphs were said to play. Their language
reflects the delicacy of the pure white flower
which does not open until midday then retires
in early evening.

# ACKNOWLEDGMENTS

*Birmingham Museum and Art Gallery*:
Page 25 Le Reveil : Jean Francois Raffaelli.

*Bridgeman Art Library*:
p2 Portrait of a girl in a blue cloak : Emma Sandys/Private Collection ;
p13 The Baths of Caracalla : Sir Lawrence Alma-Tadema/Private
Collection ; p23 Truly the light is sweet . . . : John Byam Liston Shaw/
Private Collection ; p30 La Primavera : Walter Crane/Roy Miles Fine
Paintings ; p31 A Dinner of Herbs : George William Joy/Oldham Art
Gallery ; p33 Sweethearts : Frederick Morgan/A & F Pears Ltd., London ;
p37 Love's Shadow : Anthony Frederick Augustus Sandys/Christies,
London : p43 Arranging Flowers : Edgar Bundy/Eaton Gallery, London ;
p44 The Garden : Alfred Parsons/The Trustees of the Royal Watercolour
Society, Bankside Gallery, London ; p45 Il Penseroso : Sir John Everett
Millais/Private Collection ; p47 Sir John and Lady Strickland : Arthur
Devis/Ferens Art Gallery, Hull ; p50-51 In the Garden : Frederick
Jackson/Christopher Wood Gallery, London ; p52 Song without words :
George Handel Lucas/Roy Miles Fine Paintings ; p53 Reading the letter :
Peter Kraemer/Josef Mensing Gallery, Hamm-Rhynern ; p54 Girl in a
chair : Abraham Soloman/Forbes Magazine Collection, New York ; p56-57
Spring : Lucas van Valkenborch/Private Collection ; p58 Lilac : Davidson
Knowles/Christopher Wood Gallery, London ; p59 The Bunch of Lilacs :
James Jacques Tissot/Christies, London ; p64 The March Marigold :
Edward Burnes Jones/Piccadilly Gallery, London ; p66 The Mirror :
Florent Willems/Galerie George, London ; p67 Infanta Isabel Clare
Eugenie : Alonso Sanchez Coello/Rafael Valls Gallery, London ; p71 The
Widow : James Jacques Tissot/Roy Miles Fine Paintings ; p76-77 I am
half-sick of shadows, said the Lady of Shalott : Sidney Harold Meteyard/
The Pre-Raphaelite Trust ; p87 Roses in a basket : Jan van Steensel/Gavin
Graham Gallery, London ; p88-89 The Roses of Heliogabalus : Sir
Lawrence Alma-Tadema/Private Collection ; p99 The Artist's garden at
Vetheuil : Claude Monet/National Gallery of Art, Washington.

*Christopher Wood Gallery*:
p79 Study of Phlox : George Samuel Elgood

*E.T. Archive*:
p61 Convent Thoughts : Charles Allston Collins/Ashmolean Museum

Fine Art Photographic Archive :

p7 Birthday Greetings : Raimondo De Madrazo ; p11 The Pet Bunny :
James Thomas Watts ; p12 Anemones : Annie Feray Mutrie ; p14 The
Bluebell Wood : Charles Haigh-Wood ; p15 The Swallow Track : E.
Richardson ; p18 Carnations : Emile Vernon ; p19 A Dark Beauty : Charles
Sillem Lidderdale ; p21 Carnations and Roses : Eugene Henri Cauchois ;

# PENHALIGON'S VIOLETTA

*T*HE Language of Flowers has been scented for your pleasure with Violetta. The Victorians were very fond of violets and flower sellers with baskets full of the small purple bunches were a common sight on the streets of London.

Ever since the time of the Ancient Greeks the Violet has been recognized as something rare and desirable. That they are still in such demand today gives us an indication of the true worth of this modest flower with its powerful scent.

*Sheila Pickles*

Published in the United States by Harmony Books,
a division of Crown Publishers, Inc.,
201 East 50th Street, New York, New York 10022

Published in Great Britain by Pavilion Books Limited

HARMONY and colophon are trademarks of
Crown Publishers, Inc

Manufactured in Hong Kong

Library of Congress Catalog Card Number 89-080788

ISBN 0-517-57460-8

10 9 8 7

For more information about Penhaligon's perfumes,
please telephone London 836 2150 or write to :
PENHALIGON'S
41 Wellington Street
Covent Garden
London WC2